Hunting and Safety

Annie Wendt Hemstock

PowerKiDS press.

New York

Published in 2015 by The Rosen Publishing Group, Inc.
29 East 21st Street, New York, NY 10010

First Edition

Editor: Amelie von Zumbusch
Book Design: Greg Tucker
Book Layout: Joe Carney
Photo Researcher: Katie Stryker

Photo Credits: Cover Steve & Dave Maslowski/Photo Researchers/Getty Images;
p. 4 Dana Neely/Taxi/Getty Images; p. 5 Jay Petersen/Shutterstock.com;
p. 6 Julien_N/Shutterstock.com; p. 7 Wichita Eagle/McClatchy-Tribune/Getty
Images; p. 9 Kirk Geisler/Shutterstock.com; pp. 11, 12 Jupiterimages/Photos.com
/Thinkstock; p. 13 Premium/Universal Images Group/Getty Images; p. 15 Debra Rade
/iStock/Thinkstock; p. 17 oticki/iStock/Thinkstock; p. 19 David H. Lewis/E+/Getty Images;
p. 20 Fuse/Thinkstock; pp. 21, 29 Steve Oehlenschlager/Shutterstock.com; p. 23 Chris
Williams/iStock/Thinkstock; p. 25 Monkey Business Images/Shutterstock.com; p. 27 Verity
Johnson/iStock/Thinkstock.

Library of Congress Cataloging-in-Publication Data

Hemstock, Annie Wendt.
 Hunting laws and safety / by Annie Wendt Hemstock. — First edition.
    pages cm. — (Open season)
 Includes index.
 ISBN 978-1-4777-6725-2 (library binding) — ISBN 978-1-4777-6726-9 (pbk.) — ISBN
978-1-4777-6727-6 (6-pack)
 1. Game laws—Juvenile literature. 2. Hunting—Safety measures–Juvenile literature.
3. Firearms—Safety measures—Juvenile literature. I. Title.
 SK354.2.H46 2015
 799.2—dc23
                            2014002358

Manufactured in the United States of America

CPSIA Compliance Information: Batch #WS14PK3: For Further Information contact Rosen Publishing, New York, New York at 1-800-237-9932

Contents

Why Are There Laws?

We have all been told to play by the rules. We follow rules at home. We follow rules at school. If we do not follow the rules, there are consequences.

Hunting is a sport we can all enjoy, but there are rules. There are laws that protect people and wildlife. There are laws that make sure animals have a sporting chance to get away. There are laws to help make sure that every hunter has a fair chance to take **game**.

Some states require hunters to wear blaze orange so that other hunters can easily see them.

Hunting laws do not only protect hunters from each other. They also protect the populations of game animals.

What happens if you break the hunting laws? You could lose your chance to hunt in the future. If you do not follow the safety rules, you could hurt yourself or another person. When any hunter breaks the rules, it gives all hunters a bad reputation.

In order to hunt legally, you may have to buy a state hunting **license**. A license gives you permission to hunt. You may have to pass a hunter safety class to buy a license. The laws are different in each state. You need to know the laws before you go hunting.

You need a Federal Migratory Bird Hunting and Conservation Stamp, also called a duck stamp, to hunt waterfowl. You also likely need a waterfowl stamp from the state in which you are hunting.

Hunting Facts

Conservation stamps are often quite beautiful. There are contests each year to see whose painting will be used on next year's stamp.

This Kansas game warden is checking a hunter's license after a hunt in the state's Greenwood County.

For some kinds of hunting, you may also need to buy a **conservation** stamp. There are stamps for **waterfowl**, turkey, and pheasant hunting. Your state may also have other kinds of stamps. The money you pay for your license and stamp helps wildlife.

Check the website of your state wildlife office for a list of places where you can buy a hunting license. They are often sold at sporting goods stores or online.

In the Bag

The hunting laws will tell you how many animals you can legally hunt. This is the bag limit. Sometimes, the limit is one animal. This is common for hunting deer or turkeys. You may be given a tag with your license. You need to put the tag on your animal as soon as you recover it. You may also need to **register** your kill.

For small game and waterfowl, there is usually a daily limit. This is how many you can take in one day. There may also be a possession limit that tells how many you can have at one time. This may include any at home in your freezer. Make sure you know the bag limits and other requirements before you go hunting.

Bag limits protect animal populations from shrinking. Some states require hunters to enter a contest, or a lottery, to win a chance to hunt animals like this moose.

Bag limits vary from state to state. They can also vary from one part of a state to another. They may change from year to year. They may seem confusing, but bag limits are necessary. They help keep animal **populations** healthy.

Before there were bag limits, hunters would sometimes take too many animals. Certain animals became scarce. If hunting is not allowed at all, animal populations can get too big. This is not good for the **habitat** or the animals.

Hunting Facts

When you register your kill, someone may take samples or measurements. These will help people learn more about the animals and their populations.

Wildlife biologists study animals and their habitats. They look at how many animals can thrive in an area. They use what they learn to help set bag limits so the population stays healthy.

It is against the law to hunt endangered animals like this Florida panther.

'Tis the Season

Each kind of hunting has its own season. The season is the period of time when it is legal to hunt. Seasons vary depending on where you hunt, what you hunt, and how you hunt. The season may be longer if there are too many animals in an area. The seasons are often set according to an animal's **life cycle**. Bear season may start after females are in their winter dens. Duck season begins after the birds gather in flocks to **migrate**.

Turkey season is usually in the fall or spring. It is against the law to hunt an animal when it is not in season.

This man is duck hunting in Vermont. Vermont has three waterfowl-hunting zones. Each zone has different seasons for hunting different kinds of waterfowl.

There may be a separate season for hunting with a bow. Bow season is often longer because it is harder to get close enough for a good shot. Make sure you know the hunting seasons for your area, your weapon, and your **quarry**.

Not all land is available for hunting. In most areas, you cannot hunt within the city limits. Many parks and recreation areas are closed to hunting. You should not hunt near roads or buildings. These kinds of rules keep people safe. Bullets and arrows can travel a long way.

There are certain lands that are set aside for wildlife. They are called wildlife refuges. Some refuges are closed to hunting because of research taking place there. Others are homes to rare animals.

Hunters may hunt only in areas where they have permission to hunt. Fortunately, there is a lot of land that has been set aside for hunters.

There are laws that protect the rights of landowners. These are called **trespass** laws. You should always ask landowners for permission before hunting on private property. Respect their wishes if they do not want to let you hunt on their land.

NO HUNTIN

Made in U.S.A.

Weapon Safety

Good hunters pay attention to more than just the laws. They are also very careful to be safe. Firearms, bows, and crossbows can be dangerous if they are not handled properly.

When handling a firearm, always treat it as if it were loaded. Keep the **muzzle** pointed in the safest direction. Keep your finger away from the trigger until you are ready to shoot.

Since this hunter is not ready to shoot, the action of his shotgun is open and cannot fire.

There may be other hunters or their dogs in the area. Use binoculars to be sure of your target. Aim only at your quarry, not at movement or sounds. Know what is in front of and behind your target. Do not shoot at an animal standing at the top of a hill. You do not know what is on the other side.

Safety is also important when you are not in the field. Make sure your gun is unloaded, but treat it as if it were ready to shoot. Learn how to hand a gun to another person safely.

When you are traveling, make sure your gun is unloaded and in a case. Clean your gun after you use it or if it has been in storage. Always make sure your gun is in good shape. If you find a problem, take your gun to a **gunsmith** for repair instead of trying to fix it yourself.

Make sure your firearm is stored safely. It should be unloaded and locked securely. Know your state laws about proper gun storage.

It is important to store your firearms safely and to lock them up when they are not in use.

Being a safe hunter is not just about handling your gun carefully. Remember, there are other hunters in the field, too. It is important that these other hunters are able to see you so that they know you are not a game animal.

Check your state's laws before buying your hunting clothing. Orange camouflage does not meet many state's blaze orange requirements.

Hunting Facts

Some hunters choose to wear blaze orange even if it is not required. They would rather be safe in case there are other hunters nearby.

If you are hunting with your dog, it is a good idea to put a blaze orange collar or scarf on it. This will make other hunters less likely to mistake the dog for their quarry.

Blaze orange, or hunter orange, is very bright and easy for other people to see. Many game animals, like deer, see things differently than we do. Their eyes are different from ours. To them, blaze orange is not bright, so they do not notice the color. Most states have laws that require blaze orange clothing for certain kinds of hunting. If you are sitting very still, even animals that can see blaze orange will come close. It is your movements that give you away.

Expect the Unexpected

Unexpected things sometimes happen on hunting trips. The weather might change. You might get lost or hurt. Planning ahead can help you get back home safely.

Make sure you know how to use any gear you take hunting. If you are hunting from a tree stand, make sure you know how to set it up properly. Use a safety harness to keep from falling.

Always bring the right gear on a hunting trip. Many hunting seasons take place during cold months, so dress warmly!

Let people at home know where you will be hunting and when you plan to be back. Bring water, matches, and a first-aid kit. If you are hunting in an area you do not know well, bring a map and compass or a GPS. A cell phone will let you call for help if something goes wrong.

Hunting Facts

A global positioning system, or GPS, uses satellites to find your exact location. It can help you find your way. It can also help people find you if you are lost or hurt.

Plan for a Safe and Successful Hunt

One of the best ways to prepare for your first hunting trip is to take a hunter education class. Most states require that hunters pass one of these classes before they can buy licenses.

In a hunter education class, you will learn about guns. You will learn shooting skills and how to handle a gun safely. Your teacher will tell you about the skills you will need when you are out hunting. You will also learn about what it means to be a responsible hunter.

Your state's website is a great place to learn more about your local hunting laws.

There are also classes for bow hunters. You will learn what you have to do differently if you hunt with a bow instead of a gun. A hunter education class will teach you skills that will last you a lifetime.

Once you have learned the basics, it is important that you practice what you have learned. The more you practice, the better your hunting skills will be. The more you practice, the more comfortable you will be handling a gun or bow. You will become a better shot, more able to hit where you aim.

It is also important to learn about your quarry. Spend time before hunting season starts getting to know the area where you will be hunting. This is called scouting. Sit quietly and watch the animals to learn their habits. Learn where they go to hide and where they go to eat. Practice following their tracks. The more time you spend scouting, the better prepared you will be when hunting season starts.

Hunters can pass the time between seasons by practicing shooting. This makes them better shots and safer hunters.

A Tradition for the Future

There are some people who do not like hunting. They are concerned when they hear about hunting accidents. They worry that hunters will kill too many animals.

Hunting laws and safety rules are there to make sure these things do not happen. Hunting keeps game populations healthy. The money you spend on your licenses and stamps helps wildlife. It helps protect habitat and pays for research.

Good hunters respect wildlife. They want to make sure that animal populations stay healthy. For many hunters, the time they spend outdoors is just as important as taking game. When you follow the laws and hunt safely, you set a good example. You help people see that hunting is a tradition that should continue.

Obeying your state's hunting laws and bag limits will protect other hunters and the populations of game animals.

Happy Hunting

- ⊕ Always know the laws before you go hunting.

- ⊕ Before hunting season, practice wearing your hunting clothes so you will be familiar with how it feels to move around in them.

- ⊕ Make sure to plan for a change in weather. Will you be ready if it gets cold?

- ⊕ Do not climb into a tree stand carrying a gun or bow. Use a rope to pull it up to you. Make sure your gun is unloaded!

- ⊕ If you are not required to wear blaze orange, be especially watchful for other hunters. They could be very hard to see.

- ⊕ Know the range of your gun or bow. Never take a shot that is out of range.

- ⊕ Be patient and alert. You may hear game before you see it.

- ⊕ Never shoot unless you are sure of your target.

- ⊕ Do not take a shot if there is a good chance you will not be able to recover the animal.

Glossary

conservation (kon-sur-VAY-shun) Protecting something from harm.

game (GAYM) Wild animals that are hunted for food.

gunsmith (GUN-smith) A person whose trade involves the making or repairing of firearms.

habitat (HA-buh-tat) The kind of land where an animal or a plant naturally lives.

license (LY-suns) Official permission to do something.

life cycle (LYF SY-kul) The stages in an animal's life, from birth to death.

migrate (MY-grayt) To move from one place to another.

muzzle (MUH-zel) The open end of a firearm's barrel.

populations (pop-yoo-LAY-shunz) Groups of animals or people living in the same place.

quarry (KWOR-ee) Something that is being hunted.

register (REH-jih-ster) To put something officially on a list.

trespass (TRES-pus) To enter land without the owner's permission.

waterfowl (WAH-ter-fowl) Ducks, geese, swans, and similar waterbirds.

Index

B
birds, 12

C
chance, 4–5, 30
class(es), 6, 24–25
consequences, 4

G
game, 4, 8, 28
gunsmith, 18

H
habitat(s), 10–11, 28
hunter(s), 4–5, 10, 16–17, 20,
    24–25, 28, 30

hunting, 4, 6–8, 10, 12–14,
    21–22, 24, 28, 30

K
kill, 8
kind(s), 7, 12, 14, 21

L
life cycle, 12

M
muzzle, 16

P
permission, 6, 15
population(s), 10–11, 28

Q
quarry, 13, 17, 26

R
reputation, 5
rules, 4–5,
    14, 28

S
sport, 4
state(s), 6–7, 10,
    21, 24

W
website, 7
wildlife, 4, 7, 14, 28

Websites

Due to the changing nature of Internet links, PowerKids Press has developed an online list of websites related to the subject of this book. This site is updated regularly. Please use this link to access the list:
www.powerkidslinks.com/os/laws/